Wicca for Beginners

A Guide to Wiccan Beliefs, Magic and Witchcraft

by Sophie Welch

Introduction: What is Wicca 4

    What Wicca is NOT 6

    History of Wicca 8

Chapter One: Basic Principles and Practice of Wicca 9

    1. Reverence for Nature 9

    2. The Goddess and God 12

    3. The Elements 12

    4. Magic and Witchcraft 13

    5. The Wiccan Rede 15

Chapter Two: Deities and the Divine 18

    Honoring the Deities 20

    Part 1: The Goddess 23

    Part 2: The God 25

Chapter Three: The Wheel of the Year 28

    The Days of Celebration 29

Chapter Four: The Elements 37

    Earth 38

Air 42

Fire 46

Water 50

Spirit 53

Chapter Five: Witchcraft and Magic 59

Part 1: Magic and Science................................59

Part 2: The Tools 61

Part 3: Rituals and Altars.................................65

Chapter Six: Tips for Getting Started on the Wiccan Path...68

Practicing Wicca in Secret 73

Glossary...77

Frequently Asked Questions 80

Conclusion 83

Introduction: What is Wicca

Do you feel a connection with nature on a deep, spiritual level? Do you feel peace and wonder when you step outside and walk among the plants and trees? Do you feel that all living things hold value on a physical, emotional and spiritual level? If you're looking to find a religion or spiritual practice that worships nature without specific rules or conforming restrictions, consider reading on to learn about the religion of Wicca.

Wicca is a neo-pagan ("new pagan") religion based around the worship of nature and the forces of nature that can be both magical and divine. Wiccans celebrate and honor the cycles of nature and regard all forms of life as equal. Along with plants and animals, the unifying spirit centered in the Wiccan religion exist in mountains, rivers, rocks and all of the world's natural features. This divine spiritual energy, sometimes called the Divine, exists in all things, including humans. Collectively, these concepts drive home the idea that we are a part of everything and everything is apart of us.

Wicca exists in many forms and variations for specific belief systems. For example, different branches of Wicca include Gardnerian, Alexandrian, Dianic, British Traditionalist, to name a few. I will be covering the fundamental components of the Wicca religion that encompasses the core aspects of Wicca, with a focus on the solitary practitioner.

The first thing to know about Wicca is that it can be adapted to your individual beliefs; there's no central authority and you are the one in control with the freedom to make your own decisions. After acknowledging traditional ways to practice the Wiccan religion, you are free to have your own personal perspectives and interpretations.

What Wicca is NOT

Wicca is not a devil-worshipping religion. The devil or Satan is not a Wiccan concept and does not exist in Wiccan beliefs. Most Wiccans strive to make positive, healthy decisions throughout their lives because many believe in karma or the Rule of Three (what you give you get back three times, whether that's something good or bad). There's no fear of hell to dominate Wiccan lives; just the motivation to make an active choice to do good for the sake of releasing positive energy and doing what's right on their own accord.

Wicca is not hateful, spiteful or evil. Wiccans do not sit in darkness and make animal sacrifices; that is a myth inspired by historic misconceptions spread to deter people from pagan practices. Wiccans embrace and respect both shadow and light, death and life. Wiccan ideals are built on balance, peace and love for all living things, not malicious intent.

Finally, Wicca is not always an old woman hunched over a cauldron holding a broom. Anyone of any age, gender, race or background can become a Wiccan. Avoid relying on Hollywood stereotypes to make assumptions about pagans; many witches and Wiccans lead normal lives just like everyone else, with a day job, kids and bills. Not all Wiccans are "good" or "bad" people, just like not all Christians are "good" or "bad". The pagan community is extremely diverse and no one person is the same as another.

History of Wicca

Wicca originates from much older pagan religions first developed in England in much earlier civilizations. These ancient pagan beliefs centered on worshipping the natural cycles of the earth. This makes a lot of sense because, before advanced technology, people had to rely on the seasons, the weather and the ever-changing biology and geology of the land for their very survival. To this day, seasonal cycles are still significant for crop harvest and magical work (we'll be discussing this in more detail later on).

In 1951, Wicca was introduced to the public by a British civil servant named Gerald Gardner through his books and teachings. Wicca had already been in development from pagan roots, but Gardner was one of the first people to start founding the Wicca community. To this day, Wicca continues to evolve and grow along with its practitioners.

Chapter One: Basic Principles and Practice of Wicca

In order to begin to truly understand what Wicca is and what it means to be a Wiccan, you should first learn about the following basic principles of Wicca:

1. Reverence for Nature

The word "pagan" has many different meanings. For the definition of Wicca, pagan refers to someone who practices and believes in spiritual, religious or community nature worship. Again, the word "nature" can also have many meanings. In this case, nature is all lifeforms (biologically and geologically) that make up the natural world. This usually excludes civilization and human activities, but NOT humans themselves. Humans are a part of nature, not separate from it.

Many Wiccans and pagans feel a kinship with trees, animals and rocks. The idea is that we are all connected on a scientific, physical level as well as a spiritual, divine level. Just as the earth's ecosystems connect biological and geological forms and features together, there is also a spiritual or magical force that unites all of us, making us timelessly equal and intertwined. Based on this concept arises a great respect and love of nature. Wiccans may celebrate and honor nature by some of the following actions and ideas:

Respecting all lifeforms and refraining from maliciously harming others, from flowers to insects to forests. Some practice nature worship by being vegan or vegetarian while others simply live sustainably and ecologically conscience (for example, using all parts of animals for food and practicing eco-friendly farming). The way you honor nature is up to you, as long as you remain respectful and take the time to understand the natural cycles of the earth.

Volunteer or donate to local parks and wildlife centers. These are places that work to protect animals and preserve their natural habitats. By volunteering, you'll be putting in your physical and spiritual energy toward a cause that directly benefits nature.

Plant a bee garden. Bees, including honey bees and bumblebees, provide incredibly important ecosystem services. They help pollinate a large percentage of the food that we eat, so giving back to them by planting a bee garden is a great way to honor nature and the services of bees.

Practice sustainable living, including recycling and using less resources. By doing more for the environment, you can show your gratitude to the earth and help to preserve its resources for future generations.

Walk or bike instead of drive. Even the smallest difference in carbon emissions from your car can contribute to lowering global emissions. While it may not feel like you're making much of a difference, there's plenty of other benefits to walking or biking (for one, you get to be closer to nature!).

Take time to learn. Spend time with nature and allow yourself to truly understand it. Read a book about your local wildlife or natural areas and discover what there is to know about the world around you. By simply being more knowledgeable about nature, it's possible to make more informed choices about how to become a wise advocate for animals and the environment.

2. The Goddess and God

Wicca involves the worship of a God and Goddess. These figures can be viewed and interpreted in a variety of ways, but they are traditionally represented as duotheistic deities both equal and opposite in nature. They are generally seen as a unified couple, although in some cases the God is seen as the Goddess's son (this is based on the cycles of the seasons). Chapter Two discusses Wiccan deities in more detail.

3. The Elements

Along with nature, Wiccans also regard the five Elements (earth, wind, water, fire, and spirit), which represent the phases of matter as well as the different components that together make up life within and around us. They're not just the basic elemental parts of the physical world (H20, combustion, oxygen and soil), but they also represent different forms of nature, emotions and ideals.

The Elements are often depicted in the form of a five-pointed star called a pentagram or pentacle (when the star is surrounded by a circle). The Elements are frequently used in rituals and magic work as a way of engaging with magical forces to increase the effectiveness of spells. For example, a ritual may be opened or started by invoking the Elements of Earth, Air, Fire, Water, and the four corners, with Spirit being in the center or top. The Elements can also be called upon during ceremonies, such as handfasting or self-initiation rituals.

4. Magic and Witchcraft

Magic in Wicca is sometimes spelled "Magick" to separate it from the common concept of magic that you often read in books or see in movies (I will be using Magick and magic interchangeably, both referring to Wiccan magic). Magic in Wicca is the energy of nature and the Divine; it's a force that can be engaged with and even harnessed, but never fully controlled. Wiccans use magic as a tool to manifest or create changes and initiate action toward a goal. This can be as simple as casting a good luck spell or as complex as performing a spell to help you successfully change your career.

Magic is the fluid energy that flows among the physical realm but also intertwines with the spiritual world around us and within us. Simply put, Wiccans can use magic to guide change based on the choices they make. Chapter 5 discusses magic and witchcraft in more depth; you'll also learn about the tools used in rituals and spells.

A Note About Witchcraft: Witchcraft is the practice of magic involving spells and invocations; not all witchcraft is Wiccan. Witchcraft can be seen in a wide range of different religions and cultures. While someone may refer to themselves as a Wiccan and witch interchangeably, Wicca and witchcraft are NOT the same thing. Witchcraft is a core component of

Wicca, but there are also many witches who are not Wiccan at all.

5. The Wiccan Rede

The Wiccan Rede has many forms, but usually states "An it harm none, do what ye will". More clearly, it reads "As long as you harm none, do what you will". Not all Wiccans follow the Wiccan Rede, but many use the Rede as a statement of morality to help guide choices in life. The Rede doesn't necessarily mean that we can all do whatever we want as long as we don't hurt others; it's more about making the choice to avoid harming others, both physically and emotionally, and living life to the fullest. In other words, you are responsible for your actions.

The exact meaning of the Rede is often debated among different Wicca communities. Spend some time meditating on the concept of the Rede and interpret it as you see fit based on your personal preferences and morals. The general idea is that you actively make choices that are good and moral, but you also have pure freedom to live your life as you choose.

Worth noting here is also the Rule of Three which is often brought up when discussing the consequences of magic work. The Rule of Three or Three-fold Law states that "You get back the energy you put into the world three times over". Whatever you do will come back to you later on, whether that's a positive or negative thing.

In essence, if you make positive choices, help others and contribute something good to the world, you will enjoy three times the positivity and happiness in return. Altarnatively, if you release negativity and do bad things, bad things will come back to you. Again, not everyone follows or believes in the Rule of Three.

One of the best ways to utilize the Wiccan Rede and the Rule of Three is to refer to them as general guidelines or principles, rather than restrictive, all-powerful rules. Life is always changing, and all we can do is live and find happiness the best we can without causing harm to ourselves or others.

Chapter Two: Deities and the Divine

At the core of Wiccan belief, there is a fundamental idea that within and among the world (and the universe), divine energy exists. This divine energy is commonly depicted in the form of the Goddess and the God. The definition of these figures varies among individuals, but they are essentially two dualistic figures who can manifest themselves in one or many forms. The Goddess and the God can also be interpreted as symbols for various aspects of the world. They are part of everything; not above us, but within us and around us.

The God and the Goddess may be seen as equal but opposite entities or figures, often representing masculine and feminine energies. While they are traditionally seen as male and female, that doesn't necessarily mean that they are sex or gender exclusive; it simply means that they are two parts of the same whole with opposite energies.

The relationship between the God and Goddess is usually that of divine lovers. They can be seen as the mother and father of life, as well as the dually opposite energies that exist in everyone and everything. The most important thing to remember is that they are completely equal; one does not rule over the other and both work together harmoniously.

The concept of dualism isn't exclusive to the Wiccan religion. Many other religion and spiritual practices incorporate some type of dualism (mainly, the concept of "equal but opposite figures") into their belief systems. For example, Yin and Yang from Taoism is a very similar idea of two divine figures representing opposite qualities (for example, dark and light).

In traditional beliefs, The God and the Goddess are NOT a situation of "good versus evil". Wicca ties in with the cycles of nature, and nature is far from black and white. There are aspects of both dark and light within the Goddess and the God, just as each of us have a darker and lighter side. Neither is better or worse than the other; both sides have different meanings and messages to learn from. This goes for the idea of life and death as well. In Wicca, death is not seen as something terrible and final. With death comes life and rebirth, just as leaves fall and grow again during the cycles of the seasons.

Honoring the Deities

There are several different ways you can honor and worship Wiccan deities depending on your personal choices and methods of practice. Many Wiccans simply regard the God and Goddess as dualistic forms of divine energy that lives all around us, and that's about it. Others have a more specific type of worship. For example, the God and Goddess can have many forms, including manifestations of deities from various cultures. In this case, the Wiccan would call upon that specific deity depending on what kind of spell or ritual they are performing.

In Wicca, worshipping the Divine is NOT the act of bending down in submission or expecting the gods to take full control and make all the decisions. Instead, Wiccans embrace the Divine, because the Divine is a part of what's all around us and within us, not better or more authoritative than us. Wiccans call upon deities to help advise them, guide them and assist them in making decisions and actions on their own.

If you're still wondering how you should worship the deities, or which specific deities you should worship; the choice is up to you. Here are a few ways that deities can be worshiped or acknowledged during spells and rituals:

Singing, chanting or speaking. Many Wiccans use vocal chants or sing songs to get in touch with magical energies and invoke the Divine. Physically speaking out during rituals is a great way to feel more engaged and get into the "zone" of magical work. Rhymes and chants are usually easy to remember and you can get as creative or simple as you like. Of course, not everyone likes to speak and there are plenty of other ways you can physically call on deities. Doing actions such as meditation, visualization or symbolic movements (such as lighting candles or making hand gestures) are other methods you can use.

Lighting deity-specific candles. You can have a place for the God and Goddess on your altar by simply providing them a pair of different colored candles. The colors can be whatever you feel strongest for both figures. You can also use a green, silver or white candle for the Goddess (the moon and the earth) and a red, gold or yellow candle for the God (the sun). Some believe that the placement of the candles matter on an altar, but you can arrange things according to what works for you (we'll talk more about altar arrangement in Chapter 5).

Divine symbolic tools. There are several different types of tools that can be used during spells and rituals that can help bring you closer to the forces of nature and the Divine. A cup or chalice is often used to represent the Goddess on an altar as they symbolize her womb where the origin of life occurs. For the God, a censor, wand or athame reflects a masculine or phallic presence.

Part 1: The Goddess

The Goddess may come with many names and forms, such as Mother Earth, the Moon Goddess and the Triple Goddess. When viewed as the Triple Goddess, her three aspects are the mother, the maiden and the crone; each of these forms are associated with the three phases of the moon, which is why the Goddess is often called the Moon Goddess.

Mother: An ancient mother goddess and the bringer of life. She is a symbol of fertility, sexuality, power, and life. She is seen as the full moon; ripe and swollen with stability and magical energy. You can call upon the Mother for fertility spells or spells that require a lot of power (for inner strength and fulfillment). If you're at a time in your life when you need strength and fulfilment or you'd like to get your bearings and discover your inner power, look to the Mother Goddess. The Ancient Greek Goddess Selene is a motherly figure connected with the Mother Goddess.

Maiden: The young maiden goddess represents virginity, birth, new beginnings, youthfulness, and growth. The Maiden is shown in the waxing moon, which is the growing phase of the moon as it moves from new to full. The Maiden is the representation of growing change and starting new avenues in life, such as finally pursuing your dream job or growing your family. The maiden can bring about joy, but she can also be fierce, naïve and innocent. The Ancient Greek Goddess Artemis, the virgin goddess of the hunt, is often tied with the Maiden form of the goddess.

Crone: The crone is the wise, mature form of the Goddess who carries a deep understanding of life and death. Her essence can be found in the waning moon when endings occur and lessons are learned. Like death, the Crone form of the Goddess should not be feared. She is there to guide you through the toughest of times and help you learn from your mistakes so you can put an end to things and move on. The Ancient Greek Goddess Hecate is frequently tied to the Crone; she is the goddess of herbology, magic and ghosts.

Part 2: The God

While the Goddess may seem more frequently discussed in many groups, the God is an equally important figure in Wicca. He may be referred to as the Horned God, the Sun God or he may take dual titles of the Oak King and the Holly King.

Horned God: The Horned God is the consort or husband of the Goddess, usually portrayed in the form of a wild man with horns or antlers and sometimes the head of a beast. He is the ruler of the wilderness and the symbol of virility, hunting and wild animals. His horns or antlers have nothing to do with the Christian figure of Satan; instead, they are actually symbols of his masculinity, sexuality and association with wild nature. In some Wiccan beliefs he is also aligned with death (in opposition to the Goddess, who is life). This doesn't mean he's evil, because death is not evil. He is frequently represented by the Celtic god Cernunnos, an antlered deity of animals, wealth, fertility and the afterlife.

Sun God: When speaking of the God as the Sun God, it's usually in reference to the cycle of the seasons and the Wheel of the Year. The Sun God is born from the Mother Goddess during winter (still too young but growing as the days get longer). During the springtime, he has matured into a young man who has begun courting with the Maiden Goddess, symbolizing the growth and fertility that comes with spring and the onset of new life. During the summer, the Goddess and the Sun God are wed and the God begins to mature to his peak strength when the days are at their longest. During the fall, the Sun God begins to grow tired and the days grow shorter. In the meantime, the Goddess is pregnant with the Sun God and ready to give birth during the winter, continuing the cycle all over again. Each stage in the seasons is indicated by sabbats and esbats that Wiccans may celebrate to honor the earth's changes and the cycle of the Sun God and Moon Goddess (more on this in Chapter Three).

Oak King and Holly King: Like the Sun God, the Oak King and Holly King titles are tied in with the changes of the seasons. In some Wiccan lore, there is a story about two brothers, the Oak King and the Holly King, who battle with one another. The Holly King takes hold of the throne in the winter and the Oak King reclaims his rule in the summer, with their battles taking place at Midwinter and Midsummer. The cycle continues eternally as the two bring balance to one another, a symbol of how the seasons cycle across the earth in a continuous process of birth, death and rebirth.

Note: There can be hundreds of different forms and interpretations of both the Goddess and God; the variations discussed here are only some of the primary titles.

Chapter Three: The Wheel of the Year

The Wheel of the Year refers to the continuous cycles of the earth's seasons, the sun and the moon. With the Wheel of the Year, there are eight different days of celebration, often called seasonal festivals or Days of Power. These eight days are referred to as Sabbats because they are timed with the journey of the sun and the Sun God.

Since ancient times, people have relied on the rhythms of the earth to regulate the growth of food from seasonal harvests and plant growth. Seasonal changes also dictate the cycles of reproduction in animals. In Wicca, this is tied with the cycle of the Sun God who is born from the Goddess in winter, unites with the Goddess in the spring, matures in the summer and dies in the winter. The story of the God and Goddess is highly symbolic of the way ecosystems change naturally throughout the year.

Wiccans may also celebrate Esbats, which are rituals associated with the moon. Esbats are the thirteen lunar cycles in the year that occur during the full or new moon. These are very powerful times to perform magic work, with full moons the best for spells that require lots of power and new moons best for initiations and new beginnings. Other moon phases are important as well. To celebrate annual Esbats, it would be helpful to have a lunar calendar so you can time your spells and days of celebration according to the different phases of the moon.

The Days of Celebration

Yule or Yuletide

On circa December 21st, the Goddess gives birth to the God during the winter solstice. This is the shortest day of the year, therefore the Sun God is at his most vulnerable. While there is lots of darkness and dormancy during the winter, it's also a time for celebration because the Sun God will soon grow and the days will begin to warm, bringing new life. Winter itself is also appreciated as it's a time of rest and recovery.

Dates: December 21st or 22nd in the Western Hemisphere and June 21st in the Southern Hemisphere

Symbols: Pine, holly, mistletoe, frankincense, cedar, wreaths

Celebration Ideas:

Burning a Yule log. The Yule log represents the rebirth of the God with the ignited flame.

Exchanging gifts. Gift exchange is common at this time as a way of celebrating the birth of the Sun God and the coming of spring.

Decorations. Decorate your house and Yule tree with oranges, apples, cranberries, rosebuds, cinnamon sticks and so on.

Imbolc

The Goddess is now recovering from the God's birth, with the Sun God as a young and growing boy. As the first signs of spring occur, seeds begin to sprout from the earth and the days grow longer.

Dates: February 1st or 2nd in the Northern Hemisphere and August 1st in the Southern Hemisphere

Symbols: Blackberries, ginger, rowan, willow, swans, white crystals, snowflakes

Celebration Ideas:

Lighting torches and candles. This is a symbolic activity for melting away the snow and inviting spring to come forth.

Ostara (Vernal Equinox)

The Goddess, now in the form of a fertile maiden, spreads her fertility across the earth as plants and animals reproduce and give birth or germinate. The God is beginning to mature and grow stronger.

Dates: March 21st or 22nd in the Northern Hemisphere and September 21st or 22nd in the Southern Hemisphere

Symbols: Eggs, seeds, spring flowers, hares

Celebration Ideas:

Collecting flowers. Picking wildflowers is one tradition of Ostara as a way of enjoying spring's fresh spirit (just be sure to thank them).

Planting seeds and herbal work. This is the perfect time to begin working on magical or medicinal gardens.

Beltane or May Day

As spring goes on and the days become even warmer, the Goddess and the God fall in love and unite. The Goddess is now pregnant with the God again, symbolizing the turn of the seasons as summer draws near.

Dates: April 30th to May 1st in the Northern Hemisphere and October 31st to November 1st in the Southern Hemisphere

Symbols: Bonfires, spring flowers, honey, antlers, swords

Celebration Ideas:

Making a Maypole. Erecting a Maypole and surrounding it with fresh flowers is a presentation of the sexual union between the God and Goddess.

Handfasting. As this is a time of love and fertility, many Wiccans choose to have Wiccan ceremonies around Beltane.

Litha (Midsummer)

Litha or midsummer is a powerfully magical time when the God and Goddess are both mature and rich in love and health.

Dates: June 21st or 22nd in the Northern Hemisphere and December 21st in the Southern Hemisphere

Symbols: Bonfires, oak, herbs, sunflowers

Celebration Ideas:

Bonfires. This is a popular time for enjoying outdoor bonfires in celebration of health and love.

Magical work. This is a powerful time for spellcasting, especially for love or protection.

Lammas or Lughnasadh

The first harvest has arrived and the God is slowly losing his strength has he grows older. This is a time to enjoy the fruits of our labors, both figuratively and literally.

Dates: July 31st or August 1st in the Northern Hemisphere and February 1st in the Southern Hemisphere

Symbols: Wheat, barley, oats, corn, honey, grapes

Celebration Ideas:

Feasting and giving thanks. In this time of peak harvest, many people gather together and enjoy feasts to celebrate the earth's bounty. This is also a festival of appreciation for the nourishment that the Goddess provides.

Mabon (Autumnal Equinox)

The God is preparing to move on and enter a state of rest, while the Goddess watches and feels his presence in her womb. The earth prepares for winter.

Dates: September 21st or 22nd in the Northern Hemisphere and March 21st in the Southern Hemisphere

Symbols: Acorn, oak, wine, gourds, herbs

Celebration Ideas:

Gathering dried herbs and leaves. As the leaves fall and winter comes around the corner, dried seeds and plants are gathered to be used for ceremonial decorations or herbal magic.

Walking in nature. This is a very beautiful time of year ideal for getting outside and enjoying the last days of warmth.

Samhain or All Hallow's Eve

The God has passed, but he will be reborn again in the winter. This is a time of reflection, remembering ancestors and learning to acknowledge death as a natural process not to be feared. The barrier between the living world and the spirit world weakens, making this a good time to reminisce about those we have lost.

Dates: October 21st to November 1st in the Northern Hemisphere and April 30th to May 1st in the Southern Hemisphere

Symbols: Apples, pumpkins, pomegranates, autumn flowers, cauldrons, black candles

Celebration Ideas:

Honoring ancestors. This is a holiday for getting together with friends and family and taking time to remember those that came before us. Planting seeds or sharing pictures of lost loved ones is a common celebratory activity.

Chapter Four: The Elements

The five Elements may be perceived in a variety of ways because each element has a different meaning for different people. However, there are several general correspondences that many agree upon when it comes to the symbols and meanings behind each of the five Elements. When it comes to your personal practice, choose tools and figures that you feel belong to each element. When you follow your heart and instincts, you will enhance your inner power and ultimately strengthen your relationship with the Elements.

Earth

Earth is the solid foundation of our lives. It's the strength that holds us together and grounds us in times of chaos or stress. Earth is the rich soil under our feet, the beginnings of growth and the ultimate recycle of life into death as our bodies return to the ground. Earth can be representative of abundance and prosperity, relating to the wealth of life that can be grown from the a bountiful harvest.

The colors associated with the Element of earth are green (grass, plants and trees), brown (soil and wood), yellow (leaves and sand) and black (stone and rock). Ritual items and tools associated with earth include rock crystals, stones, salt, gems and cords.

Earth figures and animals include species associated with dry land and forests, such as wolves, bears, horses and bovines. Earth is usually tied with the North direction, the Goddess and feminine energies.

In rituals, you can call upon the Element of Earth for spells that require prosperity, grounding, fertility and luck with money or employment. To invoke Earth during ritual, bury items outside in the earth, plant flowers or draw images in soil or sand with a stick, wand or your finger.

How to Practice Earth Magic

Stones and rocks: Although different types of stones and rocks can be associated with specific Elements (aside from Earth), working with them is a great way to get in tune with Earth's power. Try using stones, rocks, gems and crystals in your magic work, prayer or simply as a charm or talisman that you take with you.

Try choosing a stone or crystal that really resonates with you and makes you feel grounded, secure or even lucky. Choose a method to bless it or charge it with magical energies. You can do this by gently and safely passing it over the smoke from a candle or incense. You could also leave it under moonlight overnight; letting crystals and stones soak in a full moon's light overnight can give it a powerful charge for enhanced magical properties. If none of that feels right, simply take the stone in your hand and meditate or think positive thoughts until you feel the stone emanate comforting warmth in your hand.

How do you choose what stones and rocks to use? Your decision is totally based on your feelings; just pick something that has personal meaning for you or draws you in. Examining rocks at a nearby river or stream is another engaging and natural way commune with the earth and spend time out in nature. Always make sure to follow local laws regarding rock collection (you may need to have a permit to take them home). It's best to enjoy and leave them out in nature where they're supposed to be; the earth will thank you for it and your spells will be that much more powerful! To shop for safe and affordable stones and crystals, check out your local new age shop and find something that calls to you.

Drums and cords: Sacred drums and personalized cords are a few tools you can use to embrace the Earth Element during meditation or magical practice. Listening to the deep, rich rhythm of a handmade drum or tying sacred knots with cords in different colors and patterns is not only emotionally therapeutic, but also spiritually satisfying. Imagine the pounding of the drum as the slow, powerful beat of the earth and picture the cord as the earth's binding strength that unites us all.

Gardening: If you feel a strong connection with the Element of Earth, one of the best ways you can practice and celebrate Earth magic is by gardening. There's nothing that feels more earthly than digging your fingers into dirt, planting the roots of flowers and growing your own vegetables straight from the soil you worked with your own hands. Even if you have no outdoor space for gardening, you can still buy indoor herb gardens and house plants to tend to (make sure to choose pet-friendly versions if you have animals in your household). In return for your love and care, plants will provide you with cleaner air and nutritious or aesthetic value.

Air

Air is the refreshing breeze that flows across our skin and makes us feel more alive. It's the energy and knowledge that we accumulate throughout our lives as we sharpen our minds through study and experiences. Air is the wisdom and intelligence passed down between generations that sparks our creativity and connects us all together. Air can also be associated with psychic powers, wishes and telepathy.

The colors for Air are yellow (brightness), pale blue (clear sky) and sometimes gray (clouds). Feathers, fans, incense and wands are all magical tools frequently associated with air. Musical instruments, such as flutes or harps, can also be used to involve the Element of Air as they symbolize intellect and energy. Animal figures connected with Air are avian species such as eagles and songbirds or insects such as dragonflies or bumblebees. Air is usually more closely related to the God, masculine energies and the East direction.

Calling upon Air during magic work is great for spells that involve divination, the desire for freedom, academic success or safety while traveling. To perform a ritual associated with air, you can gently toss objects in the air, use a fan or feather to wave through the air or try calming breathing exercises.

How to Practice Air Magic

Musical instruments. When playing a wind instrument, you are using physical air as well as embracing the Element of Air by producing fresh, auditory tunes. Even if you're not very good at any instruments, just practicing with a few notes is enough to engage with Air and get your spiritual juices flowing.

Feathers and wands. Using feathers and wands in Element magic or rituals is a great way to call in the Element of Air. Keep in mind that you should not pick up feathers out in the wild as there are several laws restricting the take of feathers that could belong to endangered bird species. Instead, use feathers from domesticated bird species without restrictions, such as chickens, geese and turkeys (always refer to your local laws for specifics). Keeping at least one feather on your altar is a beautiful way to honor Air. You can also use the feather to cleanse the space and fan incense smoke during rituals. Similarly, wands are another Air-inspired addition to your altar. Wands can also be used as magical projectors or amplifiers in any kind of magical work.

Traveling. Visiting wide open spaces, such as rolling, grassing fields or open beaches, is a great way to appreciate the Element of Air and get a dose of freshness. These places can be very cleansing for the spirit. If you stand against the breeze, imagine it rushing through you and carrying away all of your negative energy and dark thoughts. Allow it to cleanse you and relieve you of unnecessary emotional weight.

Fire

Fire is the emotion we feel when we fall in love or protect our loved ones. It's the driving force behind our choices and our willingness to get up and keep moving forward, despite our hardships. Fire is the pain we experience but ultimately benefit from as it helps to make us grow. The Element of Fire is aligned with sexuality, cleansing, destruction and inspiration.

Fire colors are red and orange (flames and lava). Objects related to fire are items related to warmth, hotness or sharpness, including candles, spices, swords and athames. Many Fire animal figures are lions or reptiles such as the snake as these types of animals are often associated with warmer environments. Fire is tied with the God, the South direction and masculinity.

The Element of Fire can be invoked for spells that involve protection, sex, strength (both physical and emotional) or the banishment of negative thoughts and energies. For fire rituals, you can use both controlled indoor (candles and cauldrons) our outdoor (campfire) flames and smoke to burn, smolder or heat objects for spells.

How to Practice Fire Magic

Candles, incense and cauldrons. The use of fire-related tools is quite common in many rituals, regardless of if they're surrounding the Element of Fire. Fire is a very powerful tool because it can burn away items, produce smoke and leave ashes behind; all of these things can be used for a variety of spells, such as love or blessing spells. For indoor witchcraft, lighting candles and burning pieces of paper inside a fireproof cauldron or cup is generally a safe way to perform Fire Element spells in a controlled setting. Always remember to use caution when working with flames and make sure not to leave burning candles in a house unattended. Some spells require that the candle burn itself out while you do other things; just be sure to keep an eye on it and keep it away from other objects that it could set on fire.

Outdoor fires are especially powerful for any type of ritual, particularly when performed under the light of a full moon. Bonfires are frequently held for different Wiccan festivals and days of celebrations. This is because the symbolism of burning wood outside under the sky is often quite powerful when it comes to celebrating the Elements as well as the Goddess and God. Again, always make sure to be careful when working with fire and always keep fire in an open space with a water source nearby. For outdoor Fire Element rituals, many Wiccans will dance, sing or chant as they circle around a bonfire or campfire. Others will simply gaze into the flames and perform visualization magic or meditation.

Spices and cooking. If you can't use actual fire, you can still use tools and objects to represent the Element of Fire. Spices, such as cinnamon and allspice can be placed in a small pouch or mixed in ceremonial beverages to represent Fire. Using witchcraft in cooking and baking to bless or ritualize different foods is also a fun and engaging way to celebrate the Element of Fire while dually helping to sustain yourself or prepare for Wiccan holidays. Rather than using sweet or creamy sauces, season your food with peppers and other spices to bring forth the spiritual energies of Fire.

Water

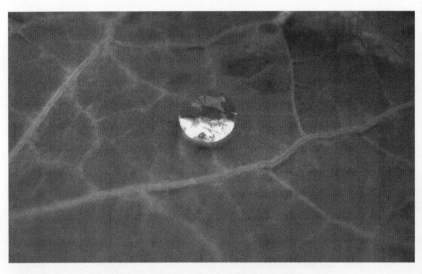

Water is the rejuvenation of your spirit when you thought all was lost. It's the hope you feel when you look into the horizon and experience emotions rise in your chest and fill your whole body. Water is seen in the healing of wounds, both physical and emotional. It can also be reflected in birth and motherhood. Water is an Element of emotions, purification, sleep, dreams and friendship.

Ritual colors for water are varying shades of blue, mainly dark blue (oceans and rivers). On an altar, Water-related items can be cups, chalices, seashells and any other objects that are able to hold liquid or relate to bodies of water. Animals connected to the Element of Water are primarily fish and marine mammals such as whales and dugongs. Water is frequently represented with the Goddess, the West direction and feminine energies.

How to Practice Water Magic

Chalices and bowls. Chalices, cups, goblets, bowls and cauldrons are all tools that can symbolize the Element of Water, regardless of if they're filled with liquid or not. Filling these items with blessed water is a great way of purifying the altar space. There are several different ways that altar water can be blessed. One way is to hold the cup or bowl in front of you and invoke the Goddess while visualizing the water in the bowl as being purified. Another powerful way to bless water is to leave it out under the light of a full moon and allow it to soak up the moon's energies overnight. If you can gather it naturally, salt water from the sea is an incredibly potent liquid for casting spells related to Water or performing purification rituals.

Potions, brews and other concoctions. Heatproof bowls can also be used for making sacred or magical brews for potions or ceremonial drinks. For example, drinking a love potion can strengthen a spell related to relationships and romance. Potions can be made from a mixture of natural ingredients, such as wine or juice, and used in rituals to become very spiritually powerful infusions. Brews are usually thicker and may even contain food items for consumption or enchantment. Witches bottles can also be filled with liquids, herbs and other items to be used for protection spells as it acts as a vessel to absorb unpleasant energies. Always remember to use natural, non-toxic ingredients when making potions and other concoctions.

Bathing and swimming. Running a sacred bath is a great method for immersing in the Element of Water and preparing for rituals by cleansing your body and figuratively washing away negative energies. The Element of Water can be an excellent source of healing, especially when accessed in wild spaces. If possible, swimming in a clear, natural lake, river or ocean can be a very powerful and sacred experience that every Wiccan should consider. Take some time to soak up the natural, wild essence of the Water Element and allow your spirit to be filled to the brim with peace and positivity. Let the waters rush over your skin and carry away any pain or fear you may be keeping locked up.

Spirit

Spirit, sometimes also called Aether, can be difficult to describe as it comes in many forms and exists in all things. Spirit is connection you experience when you walk through the forest or feel a kinship with wild animals. It's the joy you feel when your loved ones are close to you in a positive situation. It's the combination of all the elements and the eternal cycle of life and death along with reincarnation.

The color for spirit is usually white, but it could also be black or combination of various colors appropriate for each spell. The Element of Spirit doesn't have any specific animals associated with it because it can be seen in any species; some use the dove or a white stag to represent spirit in certain situations as these animals are generally a sign of peace or purity. The direction and gender for Spirit is universal and androgynous (a combination of masculine and feminine characteristics).

Spirit can be acknowledged on an altar with a white candle, but the majority of the Spirit Element will lie within yourself. Breathing softly and clearing your thoughts is one way to engage with the Element of Spirit.

How to Practice Spirit Magic

Note: The following aren't necessarily associated with any one element, but they are all activities you can do to get in touch with magical forces as well as your own inner being.

Spiritual meditation and lucid dreaming. Meditation is frequently utilized by Wiccans and non-Wiccans alike because it's an effective exercise for detaching from chaotic thoughts and stress. To meditate, you'll need a comfortable and quiet place where you won't be bothered. You can sit or lay in any position that's fairly comfortable for you (you don't want to get so comfortable that you'll fall asleep unless you're trying to do lucid dreaming). Once you've settled in, you should start to slowly inhale and exhale. Try focusing completely on your breathing.

Visualize negative energy being exhaled from your body and positive energy being inhaled. If you find yourself getting distracted, you can try saying a mantra to help you focus. At this point, you can begin to visualize yourself in places out in nature, such as a large forest. This should be a place where you can completely relax and be yourself. You may also encounter your own manifestations, such as an animal guide or spiritual manifestations of the divine.

Along with meditation, you can also try lucid dreaming by willing yourself to stay aware of your dreams even after you've fallen asleep. This can take some practice; try keeping a dream journal and concentrating on specific dreams that you can call forth and control.

Reading tarot cards. You may have heard that tarot cards are frequently used in Wicca and witchcraft for helping to make interpretations about people's lives. Tarot cards can actually come in many different forms and artwork based on a variety of themes.

Tarot cards were first developed as playing cards in 15th century Europe, but people eventually began to use them for divination. Divination is not necessarily about predicting the future, but rather being able to gain insight on a certain question or idea by interpreting the cards guided by magical or spiritual energies.

When shopping for a tarot card deck, you can either go traditional or choose something that's personalized to Wicca or nature; whatever you feel a powerful connection with will work the best.

Choose a personalized witch path. Do you feel a very powerful connection with animals or plants? Do you enjoy working with crystals and tarot cards? Are you more of a baker or chemist? No matter what your special interests may be, there are lots of activities you can try incorporating into your practice, such as:

- Gardening and herbology
- Crystals, stones and pendulums
- Alchemy, potions or aromatherapy
- Cooking and baking
- Wildlife and animal magic
- Shamanistic and healing witchery
- Sea and ocean magic
- Astrology and astral projection

These are just a few ideas for specialized activities you can do to practice witchcraft; it is NOT necessary for you to choose a specialization to become a Wiccan. They are simply ways that you can practice and engage with magical energies to enhance your relationship with nature and the Divine.

At its very core, Wicca itself is not about crystals, herbs or any physical items. Rather, it's a religion that's about finding the path that is right for you in life, living in tune with nature and the cycles of the earth and acknowledging the spiritual connection in all living things. In fact, Wicca doesn't require anything physical from you at all, and that is why you can practice Wicca however you choose.

Chapter Five: Witchcraft and Magic

Part 1: Magic and Science

While definitions vary depending on who you talk to, true magic in Wicca is the complete combination of personal power, nature power and Divine power. It's our inner spirit, the science of the world around us as well as the spiritual energies that connect us all. These three energies intertwine with one another and make up all that there is, making us all equal and related on a spiritual level.

Most Wiccans regard science and evolution as fact; after all, nature is at the heart of science and to worship nature means acknowledging the dynamic ways that nature has evolved and continues to evolve, from the smallest microscopic organisms to the largest whales in the ocean. Many agree that even Wiccan magic works with science because dealing with magical energy is all about dealing with a combination of mental, physical and spiritual power.

It's about using the strength of our minds and the forces of nature, which are fluid and ever-changing.

Magic is seen every day in the world around us, because it's also tied with the wonder of nature and life itself. For example, one might experience a feeling of magic when watching the sunrise on the edge of a cliff while feeling the first rays of the sun on their face. Magic can also be in the birth of a child, the smile of a lover or the breath of a wild wolf that's never laid eyes on a human. Science is involved, of course; there's a science to the sunrise, to birth, to love and ecology. There's no reason to say that magic is absent from these things. For people who have felt it personally, magic is as natural as the rain or the ground beneath our feet.

Wiccan practice is not founded by meaningless fantasies of things that don't exist. The real essence behind Wicca is worshipping things that are more real than anything else; life forms, their behaviors and the energies that flow within them and around them. As a Wiccan, one of the absolute best things you can do for nature is take the time to truly understand it; not just acknowledging the butterflies and baby animals, but also the predators and natural disasters that occur and make up the real processes of ecosystems and environments.

Part 2: The Tools

These are just a few of the many tools that Wiccans use in spells and rituals. None of them are absolutely required, but they all have a unique purpose for magic and honoring the Divine.

The Pentacle (Protection and Earth): The pentacle is a powerful tool that's usually placed in the center of an altar to act as a source of protection and stability. While it can represent the Element of Earth, it can also represent all the Elements and can act as a source of altar cleansing.

The Chalice and Bowls (Ritual Liquid and Water): A chalice is a cup or goblet that's used to hold water, wine or other types of potions. It can also represent the Element of Water. Other containers and bowls can be placed on the altar to hold blessed water, salt, herbs and other spell ingredients.

Censor and Incense (Cleansing and Air): A censor or incense holder are tools for lighting sticks of incense to produce a cleansing energy around the altar. Different spells may call for different types of incense, but you can usually choose whatever scent you prefer the most. Incense also represents the Element of Air.

Candles (Symbols and Fire): Candles are incredibly versatile tools that can represent just about anything. Candles can be found in just about any color you can imagine and play a vital role in spells for luck, protection, love and more. A red candle is also a strong symbol of the Element of Fire.

The Wand (Directing Energies): Wands are used to direct energies during rituals. They can be made from a variety of natural materials, such as wood, antler or bone. They're often endowed with crystals meant to imbue them with powerful magical properties.

The Cauldron (Ritual Work): Cauldrons are used to hold a variety of items that may be too large for smaller bowls, such as crystals and candles. Cast iron or fireproof cauldrons can also be used for burning or smoldering ritual items and making brews and potions.

The Broom (Managing Energies): A small broom can be kept on or next to an altar and used to sweep the altar. Not only does this help keep away dust, but it also aides in clearing away negative energies.

The Bells (Ritual Markers): Small bells can be rang to symbolize the beginning and ending of rituals. Bells can help to solidify spells, although you can also blow out candles or make verbal markers for ending rituals instead.

Crystals (Energy Amplifiers): There's a huge variety of crystals that come in all shapes and sizes from different sources; they are very powerful tools that can be used to amplify different spells or energies.

Personal Items (Spirit): Some Wiccans like to have personal items on their altars to represent themselves or honor specific figures. For example, you could have figures of your favorite animals or images of places that inspire you to help boost your spiritual energy.

The Altar Cloth (Protection): An altar cloth is a cloth or mat that goes underneath the altar to help keep things secure and organized.

The Book of Shadows (Documenting Magic Work): A book of shadows, sometimes called a grimoire, is a journal that Wiccans use to write down spells, rituals and secrets related to magic and witchcraft. Content might include notes about feelings associated with different tools, recipes for spells and potions or creative ideas or sketches. You can make your book of shadows however you wish as it's meant to be very personal and inspiring.

Part 3: Rituals and Altars

Altar Layout

Everyone sets up their altar a little differently and there is no right or wrong way to do it. You should build your altar so that it's most personal to you. It should be filled with tools and figures that you enjoy using to worship nature and deities as you see fit. However, there are a few methods for altar layouts that can help enhance the organization of the altar. Whether or not this is more effective than other methods is up for debate; again, you should go with your instincts and do what you feel is right.

Top Right (North East): God symbol. This could be a golden candle, a statue of the Horned God, an antler, an acorn or anything else you'd like to use to represent the God, or a masculine deity of your choice. A pentacle and a small bowl of salt can also be placed here to display the Element of Earth.

Top Center (North): This is an ideal spot to have a censor so that the smoke can flow over the entire altar and clear the energy around the space.

However, a stick of incense can also be placed on the middle left side of the altar to represent the Element of Air.

Top Left (North West): Goddess symbol. This could be a silver candle, a statue of the Triple Goddess figures, a special stone or anything that you associate with the Goddess or Goddess deities that you wish to honor.

Middle Right (East): This is a section where incense or feathers are placed to represent the Element of Air.

Middle Center (Center): A pentacle is an appropriate tool that should be placed in the middle of an altar, although it can also be placed on the top middle to represent the Element of Earth.

Middle Left (West): This spot is where a blue candle, cup, chalice or bowl of water may be placed. These can be used for blessings, drinking potions or representing the Element of Water.

Bottom Right (South East): This is generally where ritual knives are placed, including an athame and boline. Wands may also be placed here.

Bottom Center (South): The bottom center of your altar is where you would generally keep your spell materials, such as a specific type of candle, a piece of paper or crystals that you're currently working with. There should also be a red candle in this space to represent the Element of Fire.

Bottom Left (South West): A chalice or cauldron can be placed here depending on how much room you have.

Some people have square-shaped altars (as opposed to the circle-shape described above) with each corner having an Elemental candle, a Spirit candle on the top and a pentacle in the center. An altar doesn't have to conform to any layout and you can design it as you wish. Some people even have more than one altar, including one for magical work and another specific to deity worship. The choice is yours for however you wish to practice.

Chapter Six: Tips for Getting Started on the Wiccan Path

Now that you've been learning a little more about the Wiccan religion, you have the option of moving forward with your interest and start incorporating Wicca into your everyday life. Here are three steps to help get you started:

1. Learning. If you feel that Wicca may be right for you, one of the best things you can do to begin your Wiccan journey is continue to educate yourself about the religion. Read as many books as you can from different perspectives, keeping in mind that different authors usually have conflicting methods and information. You might also consider finding a reputable advisor or open coven that would be willing to let you witness magical work or share their wisdom. Always use caution, especially when meeting people after talking to them online. Their views and individual methods of practice may be very different from what you're comfortable with, so make sure to do your research and follow your instincts.

2. Initiation. Once you feel that you've learned and embraced the principles of Wicca, you can have an initiation ceremony. Initiation in Wicca is a rite of passage where you are "reborn" into the Craft. Initiation doesn't have to occur in a coven; solitary practitioners can initiate themselves in a variety of ways. The ceremony doesn't have to be huge and elaborate, but it can be. In its most simplistic form, self-initiation is the process of actively dedicating yourself to the God and Goddess (or Gods and Goddesses) and the Elements. In more detail, self-initiation can have the following steps:

Preparation and purification: Before initiation, many like to have a sacred bath to clean the body and calm the mind. If possible, you can anoint yourself with essential oils in a bath or lightly pat the oil on your skin. Make sure to choose natural essential oils from plants and herbs; avoid artificial oils. Play some calming music, preferable sounds of nature such as the rush of the ocean, birdsong in a forest or the soft patter of rain.

To prepare for the ritual after your cleanse, find a quiet, private place to perform the initiation ceremony.

You have the choice to perform the ritual while skyclad (without any clothes), but if that won't work for you, try dressing in fresh robes or light, comfortable clothes made from cotton or wool. The most ideal place to perform the initiation ceremony is outside under the new moon (for new beginnings), but wherever you can find that's private, comfortable and clean will suffice. Make sure the space around you is clear of any distractions. It's also best to turn off your cellphone and make sure you won't be interrupted by family or visitors.

The cleansing and preparation part of the initiation process is essential because you are clearing away the negativity from your body, mind and spirit. Of course, purification won't solve all your problems in the long-term; it is just meant to get you into a calm, relaxed state and allow you to clear your mind of clutter and stress (this goes for all rituals as well).

Invocation and verbal or mental dedication: Now that you've made your sacred space, cleared your mind and prepared your body, you can begin the initiation a few different ways. At this point, you should be completely free of any doubts about becoming Wiccan. You are about to make a vow of commitment, so it's important to feel the dedication deep within your heart, just as you would for a marriage ceremony. When you've found a quiet area (hopefully somewhere out in nature), take off your shoes and try to find a place to sit comfortably. Take a few calm, deep breaths and allow your muscles to relax. Take in the world around you. Feel the soft grass or crunchy leaves beneath your feet. Allow the breeze to caress your skin. Inhale the scents of the nearby trees. When you find yourself feeling warm and peaceful in your heart, you are ready to initiate yourself as a Wiccan.

Invoke the Divine however you see fit. You can say a small chant, or simply visualize the magical energies of nature and the God and Goddess surrounding you and protecting you. Verbally or mentally state your commitment and ask the God and Goddess to make you one with their energies so that you can feel their presence wherever you go.

Offerings and gratification: To finalize your initiation and end the ritual, it's important to give thanks to the

Divine, the Elements and nature. You can leave behind a natural offering at your altar, such as a piece of fruit. You can light a special initiation candle and allow it to burn out on its own. If you leave offerings outside, make sure they're biodegradable and safe for the environment (avoid leaving food that would attract wildlife as this could instigate unnatural behavior for them). You can get even more creative and sing a song or draw a picture for gratitude. This should be done for all rituals, not just initiation.

3. **Practice and Lifestyle**. Congratulations, you've now taken a huge step toward your journey through life following the Wiccan path! Now it's time to incorporate Wicca into your everyday life as naturally as possible. We all lead busy lives and it may often feel like we don't have any time for spellcasting, let alone having the required space or privacy. That's alright! As long as you stay dedicated to your beliefs, Wicca can be adapted for any type of lifestyle.

Practicing Wicca in Secret

Wicca is a religion based on very balanced ideals surrounding a love of nature and the enjoyment of living a fulfilled, enriched life. Unfortunately, many people have skewed or completely false perceptions of what Wicca is. Enough so that they are willing to verbally or even physically harm people who practice Wicca. If you're worried about being ridiculed or hurt by others for becoming Wiccan, there are a couple different things you can do.

If at all possible, sit down with your friends and family and explain to them what Wicca is and how you feel. Don't try to convert them; simply educate them on the general concepts and assure them that there's nothing about the religion that's evil or inappropriate. Ask them to be respectful of your beliefs, just as you are respectful of theirs.

If you're not comfortable talking to others about Wicca or doing so would put your safety at risk, that's perfectly okay. In certain circumstances for different individuals, it may be best to practice in secret until you are able to "come out of the broom closet", as it's sometimes called when a person reveals their dedication to Wicca.

In an ideal world, friends and family would accept one another no matter what religion they follow. But your safety should always come first, and you can still proudly practice Wicca even if you're unable to set up an altar or display your beliefs around others in your home. Here are a few ideas you can try practice Wicca in discretion, with or without tools:

Make a small keepsake box as your altar. Look for a small jewelry box, chest or little storage container. You can even use a shoebox or a simple wooden box from a craft or hardware store. Make sure it's small enough to keep under your bed, in your closet or wherever you feel that it would be safe and secure. Use the box as the basis for your altar. Fill it up with sacred or personal items inspired from the Goddess, God and the Elements. These can be anything from small crystals, stones and charms to written notes, tea candles, jewelry or photographs. The most important thing is that it has meaning to you and helps you connect with magical or spiritual forces. You can get out your little altar whenever you have some time for practice, meditation or spellwork. Many Wiccan spells involve lighting a candle or incense; if you can't use flame, you can use spices, unburned incense, a photo or a mental image of fire instead.

Choose a quiet, private spot somewhere outside. If you live near a park or wooded area (provided it's safe and legal to access), look for an area where you can sit down and commune with the Divine while enjoying the splendor of nature without disturbance. You don't need to have anything with you, but you could take a journal to write down your spiritual thoughts or cast visual spells with sticks, rocks and other items you find there (just be sure to give thanks and leave them where you found them).

Keep an online blog or virtual altar. While it may seem strange and counteractive to staying in tune with nature, blogging and using the internet for practicing Wicca is a growing method that works well for many people who are unable to practice in public or live in crowded cities where natural spaces are difficult to access. The beautiful thing about Wicca is that anyone can practice it however they want, so there's no reason why taking advantage of online practice won't work for certain people.

Many blogging websites are free and you usually have the choice to make them private or public. You can write entries as you would for a Book of Shadows. You'll also be able to post or share pictures that inspire you or help you perform visual spells. Being outside is always the most ideal when it comes to worshipping nature and the God and Goddess, but doing what you can with what you have is better than not being able to practice your beliefs at all.

Glossary

Athame: An athame is a blade used in magical ceremonies. It usually has a black handle and a double-edge blade, although this may vary among individuals depending on what they like to use. The Athame is used to channel magical or psychic energies. It's not really meant for cutting; instead, bolines, a type of sickle knife, are used for cutting herbs, cords and other ritual items.

The Divine: While there are many names for the spiritual energies that flow through the universe, a common term for these energies, including the God and Goddess, can be referred to as the Divine.

Handfasting: A ceremony that binds two individuals together; a Wiccan wedding. Handfasting may or may not be incorporated into a legal marriage ceremony. The idea behind handfasting is using cord or string to wrap the hands of two people together, symbolizing their eternal bond and commitment to one another.

Invocation: The process of using singing, dancing, speaking, chanting, physical action or visualization to call upon and engage with magical energies and the Divine.

Self-initiation: The process of officially asserting one's dedication to the Wiccan path. In many Wiccan traditions, Wiccans are initiated by other Wiccans in public ceremonies. For solitary practitioners, self-initiation is an equally binding ritual where they make the choice to become Wiccan. Self-initiation can be as simple as making a mental declaration of commitment; it can also take years of study and natural transition into the Wiccan practice.

Skyclad: Complete lack of clothing. Some Wiccans may work naked so that they can feel physically closer to the natural world without any barriers during rituals. If you'd like to work skyclad, make sure you are in a completely private area.

Visualization: The mental act of forming images in your mind and projecting your thoughts into visual action. Visualization is an efficient tool that can help you invoke the Divine and put your goals into action without needing to do anything with physical items. If done correctly, visualization in witchcraft is incredibly powerful and has the ability to drive major changes toward your goals by stimulating your spiritual and mental motivation.

Frequently Asked Questions

Question: What do Wiccans believe happens when we die?

Answer: There's no single answer to this question because everyone's beliefs are different, but many Wiccans believe in some form of reincarnation, afterlife and rebirth. Wiccan doesn't focus on death as an eternal end to all things because Wiccans understand that death only means new beginnings.

Question: Do we each have our own Element that we should specialize in?

Answer: The Elements are all equally present in all of us, and all of them should be respected and honored. While it's perfectly fine if you feel a closer connection with one particular Element, you should take the time to learn lessons from all five. This is often a goal for many Wiccans; mastering the wisdom of all the Elements.

Question: What are familiars?

Answer: While definitions vary, familiars are animal companions that join Wiccans and witches in magical workings. They may rub their scent on a magical tool or simply observe rituals for support. Although black cats make lovely pets, any kind of animal can be a familiar, but not all familiars need to be physical beings. Some people may have "visual familiars" that are wild animals or mythological creatures. This also touches on the realm of animal spirits and animal magic, which revolves around animals that you may feel a strong connection with or animals that enter your life in unexpected ways to teach you new life lessons.

Question: Are tarot cards dangerous?

Answer: Tarot cards offer guidance and a deeper way of thinking about things that can help us in our everyday lives. Tarot cards themselves aren't dangerous and they aren't used for communing with the dead or summoning spirits from behind the veil. Tarot cards are all about helping to explore your own inner being, not going out and seeking supernatural messages from beyond.

Question: Do I have to have an altar to practice Wicca?

Answer: The answer will probably be different depending on who you ask, but an altar isn't necessarily required for Wiccans if they are unable to have one. Wicca is about spirit, love and wisdom rather than anything physical; it's about your inner power and the power of the natural world around you. An altar is useful for having a designated space for practicing Wicca and witchcraft, which can help get you into the mindset of magical work and improve your focus. However, having an altar or not isn't the vital point of being Wiccan.

Conclusion

As you continue your journey down the Wiccan path, you'll find that there's always something new to learn. As you begin to incorporate Wicca into your lifestyle and beliefs, learn to embrace the earth's energies and hone your personalized craft methods. The more you work to understand Wicca, nature and the Divine, the more you'll continue to grow wiser and stronger in body, mind and spirit.

If you're still not sure whether or not the Wiccan path is right for you, you can start by asking yourself some of the following questions:

Do you feel that all life is connected and equal on a physical or spiritual level?

Do you feel a responsibility and love for the earth and nature?

Do you wish to seek harmony and balance within yourself and attune yourself with the natural cycles of nature?

Do you believe in the forces of magic and wish to understand the ways that magic works to help you achieve positive goals and strengthen your inner being?

The best way to know if Wicca is the best religion for you is to continue educating yourself in the principles and concepts of Wicca while staying aware of your own beliefs and perspectives. Remember that there will be a lot of conflicting information out there. Follow your heart and find a way to practice Wicca that works for you personally. If you make the active choice to embrace Wicca, it will most definitely embrace you back, just as the moon glows and the sun shines.

If you liked this book, please pay attention to my other books

Herbs and oils for beginners in Wicca with simple spells

https://www.amazon.com/dp/B0722TNLG6

Wicca: Book of spells

Would you like to **know more about Wicca spells?**

https://www.amazon.com/dp/B06XY8W8KY/

Dear Reader!

Thank you for purchasing my book! If you liked what I wanted to share with you - **please leave your feedback** on Amazon.

And I also want to share with you my new books that *you can get for free*. Subscription to new books is available at this link

www.dzenlab.com/wicca_spells/

Every time I have a new book out, you can get it for free!

Thank you!

Sophie Welch was born in San Diego and lived in the city during her childhood. Following attendance at the University of California and Los Angeles she graduated with a degree in Business.

On completion of her studies Sophie took a year out and travelled to Europe and Africa. It was during this journey that she became interested in the Pagan religion of Wicca, learning much about the subject from a community who practiced it in North Wales. From this initial interest, Sophie sought out other unusual religions and travelled as far afield as Papua New Guinea in her search, broadening her understanding as she went.

On her return to the United States she found work with an online company in New York, but soon become disillusioned by the experience and quit.

She now lives with her partner in Ohio and has devoted much of her time to writing books on religion and on her other passion of self-help.

Sophie intends to continue writing and to bring her unique views of the world to as many people as possible. In her spare time, she loves nature and taking long walks with her Labrador, Bob. She also enjoys reading, gathering and preserving nature's harvest in the Fall and spending time with the people she loves most.

Copyright 2017 by Sophie Welch - All rights reserved.

All rights Reserved. No part of this publication or the information in it may be quoted from or reproduced in any form by means such as printing, scanning, photocopying or otherwise without prior written permission of the copyright holder.

Disclaimer and Terms of Use: Effort has been made to ensure that the information in this book is accurate and complete, however, the author and the publisher do not warrant the accuracy of the information, text and graphics contained within the book due to the rapidly changing nature of science, research, known and unknown facts and internet. The Author and the publisher do not hold any responsibility for errors, omissions or contrary interpretation of the subject matter herein. This book is presented solely for motivational and informational purposes only.

Made in the USA
Middletown, DE
07 January 2019